John Bach McMaster

Outline of the Lectures of the Constitutional History of the United States

States

1789-1889

John Bach McMaster

Outline of the Lectures of the Constitutional History of the United States
1789-1889

ISBN/EAN: 9783741123856

Manufactured in Europe, USA, Canada, Australia, Japa

Cover: Foto ©ninafisch / pixelio.de

Manufactured and distributed by brebook publishing software
(www.brebook.com)

John Bach McMaster

Outline of the Lectures of the Constitutional History of the United States

Department of American History.

OUTLINE

OF THE LECTURES ON THE

CONSTITUTIONAL HISTORY

OF THE UNITED STATES.

(1789–1889.)

DELIVERED BEFORE THE SENIOR CLASS, WHARTON SCHOOL,
UNIVERSITY OF PENNSYLVANIA,

BY

JOHN BACH McMASTER,

ACADEMIC YEAR 1888–9.

Department of American History.

OUTLINE

OF THE LECTURES ON THE

CONSTITUTIONAL HISTORY

OF THE UNITED STATES.

(1789–1889.)

DELIVERED BEFORE THE SENIOR CLASS, WHARTON SCHOOL,

UNIVERSITY OF PENNSYLVANIA,

BY

JOHN BACH McMASTER,

ACADEMIC YEAR 1888–9.

THE CONSTITUTIONAL HISTORY
OF THE UNITED STATES.

PART I. 1775–1815.

--- —

I. THE REVOLUTIONARY PERIOD, 1775–1783.

I. **Civil Government taken up by the States.**

    1776. Declaration of Independence Analyzed. Colonial Government by England ended.

    1775–76. Application of the States to Congress for advice.

    1776. Congress recommends them to take up Civil Government.

    1775–78. Formation of State Constitutions.

        Analysis of the ⎫ New England States.
        Constitutions ⎬ Middle States.
        formed by ⎭ Southern States.

        Were they Republican ?
        Did the States become sovereign ?

Read Journals of Congress, Vol. I-III Poore's, Charters and Constitutions.

II. **Continental Government taken up by the Congress.**

    1. The Articles of Confederation, 1776–89.

        1776–77. History of their making.

        1777–81. History of their adoption.

        Analysis of

Read : Journals of Congress, Vol. I-VIII.

    2. Defects of the articles.

        A. In form. Acts on States and not on Individuals.
                Large vote needed to pass an ordinance.
                Impossibility of amendment.
                Plan of representation.

        B. In authority. Want of power to enforce ordinances.
                Want of Revenue powers.
                Want of Commercial powers.

ARTICLES OF CONFEDERATION.

II. UNDER THE ARTICLES OF CONFEDERATION.

Amendments asked for

1. Five per centum amendment.

    1780. Proposed by the Hartford convention.
    1781. Sent out by Congress to the States.
    1782. Ratified by twelve; rejected by Rhode Island.
    1783. Ratification of Virginia and South Carolina withdrawn.

Read: Bancroft, vol. 5, pp. 453–454, 560–561 ; vol. 6, pp. 13–14, 27–28, 33–35. Hildreth, vol. 4, pp. 427–428, 460–461. Journals of Congress.

2. Impost amendment.

    1782. Resolutions of New York.
    1783. Congress asks a specific duty and permanent revenues.
    1783–84. Specific duties granted by twelve States.
    1786. New York refuses.
    The Confederation breaks down.
        Causes of the failure.

3. The commerce amendment.

    Text of.
    1784, April 30. Amendment sent out.
    1784–87. Action of the States.

4. Failure of the Articles.

    Violated by Congress.
    Violated by the States.
    Need of coercive power.

III. FRAMING THE CONSTITUTION.

1. The Federal Convention Called.

    1782. Resolution of New York.
    1782–85. Resolutions of Massachusetts.
    1784–85. Virginia and Maryland Commercial Commission.

FRAMING THE CONSTITUTION.

1786. Virginia calls Annapolis Convention.
1786. Annapolis calls Federal Convention.
    The call approved by New York and Massachusetts.
    Virginia, New Jersey, Pennsylvania, North Carolina, Delaware.
    New York proposes that Congress call a Convention.
1787, Feb. 22. Congress issues a formal call for the Philadelphia Convention.
    New York approves.
    April. South Carolina and Georgia.
    May. Connecticut and Maryland.
    June. New Hampshire.

II. **The Work of the Convention.**

    1787. May—September. Character of the delegates.
        Powers of the delegates.
        Parties in the Convention.
    1. Great States and little States.
    2. Northern States and Southern States.
    3. Agricultural States and Commercial States.
    4. Federalists and Anti-federalists.
    5. "Centralizers" and "State-rights-men."

The Plans offered

    1. Virginia plan.
    2. New Jersey plan.
    3. Connecticut plan.
    4. Pinckney's plan.
    5. Hamilton's speech.
        Virginia plan adopted.
    1787. May—July. Discussion of the general plan.
        August— September. Discussion of details.
        The three Compromises.
    1–Representation of States.
    2–Representation of Slaves.

CONSTITUTION RATIFIED.

3–Slave trade and commerce.

September 17. Constitution signed.

Read: Curtis' Hist. of Const. Bancroft's Hist. of Const. Madison's Notes. Yate's Notes. Luther Martin's Genuine Information.

Sources of the Constitution.

    1. The State Constitutions.
    2. The Articles of Confederation.
    3. The Experience of Congress.
    4. Montesquieu.
    5. English Constitution.

III. The Constitution before Congress.

    1787. Sept. Opposed by New York delegates, by R. H. Lee, Grayson, of Va. and Nathan Dane, of Mass.

    Sept. 26. Lee moves bill of rights and amendments.

    Sept. 27. Motion to send the Constitution to the States.

    Sept. 28. Motions expunged and the Constitution submitted to the States.

IV. The Constitution before the people.

    1. Objections, By noted men.
    2. By essayists and pamphleteers.
    3. By the newspaper writers.
    4. By " Centinel."
    5. Defence of, By noted men.
    6. By pamphleteers.
    7. By newspaper writers.
    8. By " Publius."
    9. Review of " The Federalist " and " Centinel."
    10. Choice of delegates to the State Convention. Did the delegates represent " We the People " ?

V. The Constitution before the State Conventions.

    1787. Dec. 9. Delaware ratifies.
    Dec. 12. Pennsylvania.
    Dec. 18. New Jersey.

6

1788. Jan'y 2.   Georgia.
      Jan'y 9.   Connecticut.
      Feb'y 7.   Massachusetts.
      April 26.   Maryland.
      May   23.   North Carolina.
      June 21.   New Hampshire.
The Constitution adopted.
      June 26.   Virginia.
      July 26.   New York.
1789, Nov. 21.   North Carolina.
1790, May   29.   Rhode Island.

CHARACTER OF THE CONSTITUTION.

1. The Form.

    1. The Legislative department.
    2. The Executive department created.
    3. The Judicial department created.

2. The Powers granted.

    1. Increase of the powers of the general government.
    2. Decrease of the powers of the States.

3. Means of carrying out the Powers granted.

4. Powers omitted.

    1. To annex territory.
    2. To protect national elections.
    3. To prevent secession.

5. Powers not well defined.

    1. Power to regulate slavery.
    2. Power to govern Territories.
    3. Extent of power to regulate commerce.
    4. Extent of war powers.

THE TEN AMENDMENTS.

5. Extent of "general welfare" powers.
6. Extent of powers to raise and use revenue.
7. Tenure of office.
8. Power of the States.
9. Powers of the Judiciary.
10.

IV. THE CONSTITUTION IN FORCE.

1788. July 2. Constitution declared adopted by President of Congress.

September 13. Day fixed for putting it in force.

October 21. Continental Congress expires for want of a quorum.

1789. March 4. The Constitution in force.

The Amendments, 1789–1800.

1787–88. Number and character of the amendments offered by the State Conventions.

1788. New York calls a second convention.

Pennsylvania minority call a conference.

1788. Harrisburg Convention.

1789. Memorial from Virginia.

Debate on the question of amending.

Nine amendments offered by Madison.

1789. Aug. 25. House send seventeen to the Senate.

Sept. 9. Senate returns twelve.

Sept. 25. Twelve sent to the Senate.

1791. Dec. 15. Ten declared in force.

1793. Case of Chisholm vs. Georgia.

1794. March 5. Eleventh amendment offered.

1798. Declared in force.

Elliot's Debates; Adam's Life of Gallatin; Pennsylvania and the Federal Constitution; Annals of Congress, 1789–91; History of Congress during Washington's Administration; U. S. Supreme Court Reports.

POWER OF REMOVAL.

V. INTERPRETATION OF THE CONSTITUTION, 1789–1801.

I. **By Congress.**

A. **Power of Removal by the President.**

1787. Review of the history of the appointing power as discussed in the Federal Convention.

1788–89. In the amendment offered by the States does the
power to appoint include the power to remove?

1789, May 19. Madison's motion.

June 16–24. Debate in the House.

Four questions settled.

1. Appointing power does include removing power.

2. Both powers belong to the President.

3. When the Constitution does not specify the tenure of
office, the office is held at the pleasure of the appointing power.

4. Heads of departments are not "inferior officers."

Elliot's Debates; Madison's Notes; Annals of Congress, 1789–91.

B. **Power of Removal by Impeachment.**

History of the offense of Wm. Blount, of Tenn.

1797, July–Nov. Action of the House.

The trial before the Senate.

Questions raised.

Case dismissed for want of jurisdiction.

Adam's Message, July 3, 1797. Annals of Congress, 1797–98.

C. **Power to Assume State Debts.**

1790, Jan'y 14. Assumption of State debts urged by Hamilton.

March–April. Principle accepted and rejected.

July. Compromise effected by Jefferson.

Nov. 3. Virginia declares the act unconstitutional.

North Carolina resolutions.

D. **Power to Charter a National Bank.**

1790. Plan of Hamilton.

Feby. 1. Questions raised in the House.

THE NATIONAL BANK.

1. Expediency.
2. Constitutionality.

I. Arguments in the House of Representatives.

Are the details constitutional?
Is the principle constitutional?
Speech of Madison.
His rules for interpreting the Constitution.
Arguments of other members drawn from
Power to " borrow money."
Power to " lay taxes."
Power over " property."
Power to " raise armies and navies."
Power to act for " the general welfare."
Power to do what is " necessary and proper."

II. Arguments of the heads of departments.

Argument of Hamilton in defence of
Express powers.
Implied powers.
Resultant powers.
Argument of Jefferson in defense of
Express powers.
Reserved powers.
Arguments of Randolph.

III. Dissent of the States.

*Works of Hamilton ; works of Jefferson ; Annals of Congress, 1791.
Marshall, Works, 160–187.*

E. Powers of Congress over Slavery.

1787. The question of Slavery in the Federal Convention.
Compromises concerning
Constitutional provisions concerning
1. Direct taxes.
2. Right to stop slave trade.

3. Limitations on an abridgement of citizenship.
4. Duty to send back fugitive slaves.
1790. Feb. 11, 12. Memorials sent to Congress.
Feb. 16. Debate on the powers of Congress over slavery.
March 16. Report of a Committee.
March 23. Amended report entered on the Journal.

Bancroft's History of the Constitution; Elliot's Debates; Annals of Congress; Curtis' History of the Constitution.

F. **Power of the House of Representatives over Treaties.**

Constitutional Provisions Touching Treaties.
1794. History of " Jay's Treaty."
1796. March 1. Resolution calling for papers.
Question discussed.
1. What is a constitutional treaty?
2. What is meant by " supreme law of the land "?
3. Is treaty making a legislative act?
4. Can a treaty bind the House to make appropriations?
March 24. The House call for papers.
March 30. Washington refuses.
April 7. Resolutions of the House.

II. **By the States.**

A. **The Question of Usurped Powers.**

1798. Alien and Sedition Acts.
Feeling toward foreigners.
Numbers in the country.
Proposition to shut them out from office.
Third Naturalization Act, Text of.
Constitutional question of citizenship.
The Alien Friend Act, Text of.
Constitutional questions.
1. What is meant by " migration?"
2. May the executive and judicial functions be combined?
3. The personal liberty question.

KENTUCKY RESOLUTIONS.

The Alien Enemies Act, Text of.
The Sedition Act, Text of.
June 29.—July 14. History of its passage.
Constitutional questions.
1. Does it violate the guarantee of freedom of speech and of the press?
2. Does it violate the "habeas corpus" provision?
3. The question of common law jurisdiction.

Statutes at Large; Annals of Congress; Story's Commentaries, §§ *1293–1294; 1885–1886.*
1798, Nov. 19. First Resolutions of Kentucky.
Dec. 21. First Resolutions of Virginia.

Preston's Documents Illustrative of Amer. Hist. Elliot's Debates, IV, p. 540. Shaler's Hist. of Kentucky, p. 409.
1798, Answers of the States.
1799, Nov. 29. Second Kentucky Resolutions.
1800, Feb. 2. Report of the House Committee on the resolutions.
1800, Report of Madison on the answers of the States.
Pamphlet literature on the subject.
What did the resolutions mean?

B. The question of suability.

1793, Georgia *vs.* Brailsford.
Chisholm *vs.* Georgia.
————*vs.* Massachusetts.
The eleventh amendment.

III. By the President.

Powers of the President.
1. To withhold papers asked for by the House.
2. To declare neutrality.
1793, April 5. Neutrality proclaimed.
Declared unconstitutional.
Defended by Hamilton in letters of "Pacificus."
Attacked by Madison in letters of "Helvidius."

REMOVAL OF THE JUDGES.

IV. By the Supreme Court.

Review of the decisions of the Court.   1790–1800

V. Defects of the Constitution 1789-1800.

    I. Defects for which amendments were offered and not passed.
The direct tax amendment.
The anti-charter, anti-monopoly amendment.
The civil disability amendments.
The judiciary amendment.

    II. Defects for which amendments were offered, passed and ratified
by the States.
The eleventh amendment.

INTERPRETATION OF THE CONSTITUTION, 1801–1817.

I. By Congress.

  A. Power to Remove the Federal Judges.

    1801. Federal Act on the judiciary.
    1802. Reasons given by the Republicans for its repeal.
Constitutional questions involved.

  1. Freehold in office.
  2. Diminishing emolument while in office.
  3. Meaning of the word " may " and " shall."
The Act repealed.

    1803. The case carried to the Supreme Court, Marbury *vs.*
Madison.

  B. Power to Acquire Territory by Treaty.

    1801–03. History of the purchase of Louisiana.
    1803. Provisions of the treaty.
    1803. The question of constitutionality.

    I. The views of Jefferson.

    II. The Federalist arguments against the constitutionality.

  1. The call for papers.

LOUISIANA PURCHASE.

2. Treaty making power does not extend to acquiring foreign soil.
3. Meaning of " New States."
4. Preference given ports of Louisiana.
5. Attempt to regulate trade.
6. Citizenship argument.
7. Pickering's " partnership " theory.

    III. The Republican arguments in support of the constitution-
ality drawn from
    The treaty power.
    The war power.
    The power over territories.
    The " general welfare " clause.
    Effects of the purchase on the Federalists. The New
England plot. Threats of disunion.
Annals of Congress. Adam. New England Federalism.

c. **Power to lay an Embargo.**

    1807. Sketch of the events which led to the embargo.
    1807–9. Summary of the embargo laws.
    Were they constitutional ?
    Were they a " regulation of commerce " ?
    Were they an exercise of the " war power " ?
    1809. The " Force Act."
    Reasons assigned for its unconstitutionality.
    Sections 2 ; 4 ; 7 ; 9 ; 10.
    Excessive bail.
    Excessive fines.
    The right to be secure in persons and papers.
    1809. Resolutions passed by Legislatures and public meet-
ings.
    Fears of secession.

D. **Power to regulate slavery.**

    1807. Constitutional provision for the abolition of the slave
trade put in force.

14

THE WAR POWERS.

II. **By the President.**

    A. **Power to make war.**

        1802. Jefferson's views in connection with the war with Tripoli.

        Views of " Lucius Crassus."

    B. **Power of the President to fill vacancies during the recess of the Senate.**

        1802. Argument of Lucius Junius Brutus.

        Argument of Leonidas in reply.

1812. C. **Power of the President to call out the Militia.**

        April 10. Act of Congress.

        June 12. Dearborn's Order.

        Refusal of the Governors of Massachusetts, Connecticut and Rhode Island.

        Constitutional reasons for refusing.

        Question of the judge of the exigency.

        Question of delegating the powers to command.

        Answers of Massachusetts judges.

        Answer of the Rhode Island Council.

        Answer of the Connecticut Assembly.

        Case of Martin *vs.* Mott, 12 Wheaton, 19.

Niles Register ; Dwight's Hartford Convention, Story's Commentaries, §§ 1204-1206.

III. **By the States.**

    A. Growth of the States Rights Doctrine.

        1804. Effect of the Louisiana purchase on New England.

        1809. Refusal of the Governor of Connecticut to obey the President's militia order.

        Feb. Resolution of the Connecticut Legislature.

        1809. Resolution of the Massachusetts Legislature.

        1809. The Olmstead case in Pennsylvania.

        Feb. 27. Message of Governor Snyder to the Legislature.

THE FINAL ARBITER.

1809. March 1. Report on the message.
" Resolutions on States Rights.
1809. Pennsylvania calls for a constitutional amendment.
1810. Answer of Virginia.

B. Is there a final arbiter?
1798, Dec. Judge McKean's opinion (3 Dallas, 473).
1799. John Marshall's opinion.
1800. Madison's opinion.
1809. Justice Tilghman's opinion.
1811. Pennsylvania resolutions on the Bank of the United States.
1814. Lloyd's reports on interposition.
1814. Connecticut's instructions to her Governor.

IV. Defects in the Constitution. 1801-1817.
1. Defects for which amendments were offered and passed.
1880–02. Separate ballot in electoral colleges for President and Vice-President.
1800–03. Providing for choice of electors in districts.
1802. Resolutions of New York, South Carolina, and
1803. Ohio.
1803. Providing for number of Presidential terms.
1803. Twelfth amendment sent out to States.
1804. Declared in force.
2. Defects for which amendments were offered and not passed.

A. The Supreme Court.
1800. No judge to be appointed to office.
1805. Extent of judicial powers defined.
1805. Judges to be removed on joint address of both Houses.
1806. Pennsylvania amendment, limiting jurisdiction.
1807. Limiting judicial power.
1806. Kentucky amendment on the same.
1806. Vermont resolutions.
1807. Judges to hold office for —— years, and removable on address of two-thirds of Congress.

PROPOSED AMENDMENTS.

1808. Virginia resolution on the subject.
1808. Massachusetts resolution on the subject.
1808. Judges removable on address of three-fifths of both Houses.
1808. Pennsylvania resolution.
1809. Maryland disapproves.
1809. Relating to the judges.
1812–1816. Removal of the judges.

B. **Miscellaneous.**

1804. Representatives and direct taxes to be apportioned according to free inhabitants.
1806. Maryland : Migration and importation of slaves into United States prohibited after January 1, 1808.
1808. Pennsylvania resolution on the same.
1806. Government contractors not eligible to Congress.
1808. Relating to disabilities of office-holders.
1808. Choice of President and Vice-President by lot.
1810. Forbidding the acceptance of any title of nobility.
Sent to the States.
History of the Amendment.
1813. Relating to manner of electing President.

C. **Amendments affecting the powers of Congress.**

1806. Interpreting the last clause of 8th Section of 1st Article of the Constitution.
1813. Giving Congress power to lay export duty ; power to make roads in any State with the consent of the State ; power to make canals in any State with consent of that State ; power to establish a national bank.
1814. To shorten the term of Senators.
1815. Amendments offered by the Hartford Convention.
The Convention.
I. Reason for the call.
Militia.

THE HARTFORD CONVENTION.

Conscript Bill.
Impressment Bill.
The Embargo.
Addresses and violent restrictions on the war.
Refusal of the Government to defend the New England coast.

II.   The call sent out.

1814, Oct 8.   Massachusetts issues the call.
Action of Connecticut and Rhode Island.
Action in Vermont and New Hampshire.
Instructions.

Dwight's Hartford Convention ; Nile's Register, Vol. 7 ; Lodge's Cabot, 505 ; Von Holst, I, 243-272.

The Report of the Convention.

1814, Dec. 15.   Delegates meet at Hartford.
1815, Jan'y 5.   Report adopted.
1815, Feb'y.   Commissioners sent to Washington.
Mch. 3.   Report laid'before the Senate.

The seven amendments proposed.

1816.   Congress and the States concurrent power to train the militia.
1816.   Concerning the pay of Congressmen.

By the Supreme Court.

1801-1817.   Decisions of the Supreme Court reviewed.

VII.   RESULTS OF THE WAR.

The Bank question.

I.   1811.   The question of recharter.

   A.   The constitutionality deduced from precedent.

      1.   Congress has declared it to be constitutional.
      2.   The States and the people have declared it to be constitutional.

RECHARTER OF THE BANK.

B. The constitutionality deduced from the powers of the Constitution.

   1. To lay and collect taxes, duties, imposts.
   2. To borrow money on the credit of the United States.
   3. To regulate commerce, with foreign nations and between the States.
   4. To make all regulations for the territories.
   5. To make all laws necessary and proper to carry out the provisions of the Constitution.
   6. The States forbidden to issue bills of credit.

C. The unconstitutionality deduced from.

   1. The power not expressly delegated.
   2. Dangerous to admit constructive powers.
   3. Interferes with States rights.
      a. Violates the usury laws.
      b. Authorizes foreigners to hold real estate.
      c. Exempts private property of stockholders from liability for bank debts.
      d. Powers to grant charters a State right.

D. 1811. Objections of the States.

   a. Arguments of the Legislature of Pa.
      1. Definition of the Constitution.
      2. Remedy for usurped powers.
      3. Consent of the States must be had.
   b. Arguments of Virginia Legislature.

III. 1816. The question of the second U. S. Bank.

A. The old arguments of 1811 reasserted.

B. Calhoun's argument based on power of Congress to "regulate currency."

C. The particular charter unconstitutional because it violates the condition " necessary and proper."

      1. So much capital not " necessary."

STATUS OF TREATIES.
2. Government directors not "proper."
3. Interferes with concurrent powers of the States.
D. The charter granted.

VIII. CONSTITUTIONAL STATUS OF TREATIES.

I. **Review of the circumstances that brought up the question.**

1815. July 3. The convention with Great Britain.
1816. The bill to put the provisions of the treaty in force.

II. **The questions discussed.**

1. Does a treaty repeal a law ?
2. Does a treaty become a law without legislative action ?
3. Is a treaty a " law ?"
4. What is meant by " supreme law ?"
5. By " to make " treaties ?
6. By " under the authority of the United States ?"

III. **Report of the Conference Managers to the Senate.**

Annals of 14th Congress, 1st Session.

THE CONSOLIDATION OF THE UNION.

THE RESERVED RIGHTS OF THE STATES.

PART II. 1805—1833.

Effect of the War of 1812–15 on the consolidation of the Union.

STATES RIGHTS ASSERTED.

Causes of the assertion during this period.
1. Decisions of the Federal Courts.
2. Acts of Congress.

1. Decisions of the Federal Courts.

I. Asserting Jurisdiction.

1816. Martin *vs.* Hunter's Lessees.
    a. May the Supreme Court set aside a State law?
    b. May it pass on the validity of a treaty?
1821. Cohen *vs.* Virginia.
    a. Has the Supreme Court jurisdiction when a State is a party?
    b. May it reverse the judgment of a State Court?

II. Upholding Powers of Congress.

1819. McCullough *vs.* Maryland.
    a. May Congress create corporations?
    b. May Congress charter a bank?
    c. May a State tax the bank?

THE SUPREME COURT AND THE STATES.

1824. Osborn *et al. vs.* Bank of the United States.
- *a.* Is the bank a public corporation ?
- *b.* May the United States protect it against the State ?

III. Decisions Declaring State Laws Unconstitutional.

1810. Georgia. Case of Fletcher *vs.* Peck.

1819. New York. Bankrupt law. Case of Sturgis *vs.* Crown-inshield.

1819. New Hampshire. Dartmouth College case.

1819. Maryland. United States Bank tax. McCullough *vs.* Maryland.

1820. Ohio. United States Bank tax.

1821. Virginia. Cohen *vs.* Virginia.

1823. Kentucky. Certain loans of 1797 and 1812 set aside, case of Green *vs.* Biddle.

1823. South Carolina. The negro seamen act.

1824. New York. Case of Gibbons *vs.* Ogden.

1824. Georgia, Bank of United States *vs.* Planters' Bank.

1825. Kentucky. The replevin laws.

1827. Maryland. Brown *et al. vs.* Maryland.

EFFECTS OF THESE DECISIONS.

1. Attempts to amend the constitution.
   1821. Kentucky amendment giving an appeal to the Senate in cases to which States are parties.

2. Attempt to repeal the 25th section of the Judiciary Act of 1789.
   1830. Dec. 21. Committee appointed in the House. Full text of the 25th section.
   1831. Jan. 24. Majority report.

1. The Act unconstitutional.
   - *a.* The State Judiciary not created by the constitution.
   - *b.* Congress no power to regulate appeals in Courts not created by authority of the constitution, because

*THE JUDICIARY ACT OF 1789.

   c. The States are sovereign.

   d. The power to regulate their judiciary is not expressly given.

   e. The power is not incidental to any express power.

Jan. 24. Minority report.

  1. The Act constitutional.

    a. Powers the State judiciary possessed before the establishment of the constitution not interfered with.

    b. The appeal to be only in cases arising under the constitution, the laws, or the treaties.

    c. Necessary for the general welfare that the constitution be interpreted uniformly.

Jan 29. Bill to repeal rejected.

1831 Feb Debate on printing the reports.

II. Acts of Congress causing assertion of States Rights.

  1. Internal Improvements.

  2. The Tariff.

  3. Greed for government money and land.

  4. North-eastern boundary convention.

  5. The treaties.

2. INTERNAL IMPROVEMENTS. 1783–1816.

I. **1783. Propositions to use surplus of Land Sales for Internal Improvements.**

II. **Policy of the Federalists.**

    1791, Dec. 5. Suggestion of Hamilton.

    1796. Grant of land to Zane.

III. **Policy of the Republicans.**

    1802, Feb. 13. Gallatin proposes a government road.

       April 30. Five per cent. of land sales given to Ohio.

INTERNAL IMPROVEMENTS.

1806, March 29. First Cumberland road act.
1805-7-8. Jefferson proposes a constitutional amendment.
1807, Feb 10. Coast survey act.
1807, Feb. 28. Land grant bill.
1808. Gallatin's report.
1812. North and south road.

IV. **The Constitutionality of Internal Improvements.**

1. Language of the Constitution.
    " Regulate commerce * * * among the several States."
    " To establish * * * * post roads."
    " Provide for the commerce, defense and general welfare."
    " To make all laws which shall be necessarry and proper for carrying into execution the foregoing powers."

2. The Bonus Bill. Congressional action.

    1815, Dec. 5. President's message recommending construction of roads and canals.
    1816, Feb'y 6. Senate committee make a report.
    1816, Dec. 3. President again urges internal improvements.
        Dec. 16-23. Calhoun's bonus bill.
    1817, Feb'y 8. Report of committee on President's message.
        Feb'y-March. Debate on Calhoun's bill.

    A. The power to build roads and canals incidental to the power.
        1. To raise and collect armies.
        2. To provide for the common defence.
        3. To provide for the general welfare.
            a. Would cement the Union.
            b. Would aid internal trade.
            c. Would increase wealth and population.
        4. To regulate commerce between the States.
            a. Has Congress power to clear a river of dams or obstructions put up by State authority?

INTERNAL IMPROVEMENTS.

b. Has Congress power to make any water-course a highway against the will of the State in whose territory it lies?

c. The meaning of " regulate."

5. To do whatever is " necessary and proper."
6. To make all needful rules and regulations for the territories.
7. Power to lay and collect taxes.

B. The power to build roads and canals expressly granted by the clause.

1. To establish post-offices and post-roads.

C. No power to build roads or canals because,

1. The power is not expressly granted.
2. The States have reserved and use the power to make roads and canals.
3. " Post-roads " does not mean highways.

D. The question of consent of the States.

1. Does the consent of the States justify an act of doubtful constitutionality?

V. Internal Improvements. Veto of the President.

1817, March 3. Veto message of Madison.
Attempt of the House to pass the bill over the veto.

VI. Internal Improvements. The power of Congress asserted.

1817, Dec. 2. Monroe recommends a constitutional amendment.
Dec. 9. The amendment moved.

1. Congress to have power to appropriate money for building roads and canals.
2. The consent of the State to be obtained.
3. The money to be appropriated on the basis of representation in the House.

INTERNAL IMPROVEMENTS.

1817, Dec. 15. Report of House Committee on Internal Improvements in which is discussed:

1. When the Constitution should be construed strictly.
2. When the Constitution should be construed broadly.
3. The meaning of the terms " establish "; " necessary "; " proper."
4. Right of Congress to build military roads.
5. Right of Congress to appropriate money in aid of internal improvements.
6. Resolution prepared.

1818, March 6. Debate on the question.

1. Is the consent of a State necessary?
2. May a State Legislature transfer its power to Congress?
3. May Congress vote money in aid of internal improvements carried on by the States or by corporations?

March 14. Committee of the whole report four resolutions.

The House passes one, asserting the power of Congress to appropriate money for the building of roads and canals.

1822, May 4. Monroe vetoes the Cumberland Road Bill.

May 4. Long interpretation of the Constitution by Monroe in a message.

1823, Dec. 15. Bill appropriating money to procure necessary surveys or estimates for roads and canals.

1824, Jan'y. Debate on powers of Congress.

1. The old arguments used again.
2. Question of right-of-way.
3. The " private property " clause (5th amendment).
4. The question of " consolidation."

1824, April 30. The bill signed.

1825, Jan'y, Feby. Bill to extend the Cumberland road. Bill to authorize the subscription to the stock of the Chesapeake and Delaware canal.

1. The question of constitutionality not debated.
2. Status of the question.

1825, Jan'y. Protest of the Senate of South Carolina.

INTERNAL IMPROVEMENTS.

1826, Dec. 15. Motion to instruct the Committee on Public Lands to inquire into the constitutional power of Congress to use the public lands for internal improvements.

1827. Constitutional question raised by items in the general appropriation bill.

1828. Bill making appropriation for internal improvements.
1. The question discussed at length.

1828, Dec. 18. Resolutions denying Congress power to make internal improvements.
1. State sovereignty retained.
2. Rights of jurisdiction and soil are attributes of sovereignty.
3. Power to make internal improvements involves the right of jurisdiction and soil.
4. Power to make roads and canals within the limits of the States involves the right to make a complete system of internal improvements.
5. Congress does not possess this power.

1829. Bill for the repair of the Cumberland road.
1. May Congress gather revenue by tolls on the road.
a. Power to lay or collect taxes.
b. " All duties, imports, and excesses shall be uniform throughout the United States."

1829, December. Jackson's suggestion in his message.

1830, January. Bill to distribute among the States the net proceeds of the sales of public lands, to be used for purposes of education and internal improvement.

1830, March 1. Buffalo and New Orleans Road bill
Constitutional powers of Congress again discussed.
2. Maysville and Lexington Turnpike road.

1830, May 27. Jackson vetoes the bill as unconstitutional.
May 31. Veto of the Washington Turnpike bill.

1830, Dec. 7. Jackson discusses the vetoes in his message.

1831, Feb'y 25. Bill to give assent of Congress to an Act of the Legislature of Ohio concerning the national road.
Ohio asked for power.

THE TARIFFS OF 1828–32.

1. To collect a toll to be used for repairs.
2. To give justices of the peace jurisdiction over the road for the purpose of punishing persons maliciously injuring the road.

Constitutional Questions Discussed.

1. May the United States transfer to Ohio the power to collect tolls?
2. Has Congress power to collect tolls.
3. Has Congress power to give State officers authority to enforce United States laws?

3.   THE TARIFF.

The Question of Constitutionality.

1816.   The question not discussed.

1820.   The question not discussed.

1824.   The question touched on, and the right to lay protective duties deduced from.

    1.   Power to lay and collect taxes, duties, imports, excise.

    2.   Power to regulate commerce.

1825, January 13. Resolutions of South Carolina denying the right.

1828, March 4. The tariff bill taken up.

    1.   Question of constitutionality debated as before.

    December 30.   The Act declared unconstitutional by Georgia.

1829. " Unconstitutional, oppressive and unjust " by South Carolina.

1831, Feb. 25.   Benton's resolutions on

    12.   Power to lay and collect duties.

    22.   Power to regulate commerce.

1831, Sept.   Address of the Free Trade Convention.

    Address of the convention of " Friends to Industry."

1832, Jan. 9.   Clay's resolution for modification.

    McDuffie's report (the Southern scheme.)

1832, May 30.   Adams' report (the Protection scheme.)

1832, July 14.   The Act passed.

"THE SOUTH CAROLINA DOCTRINE."
4. NULLIFICATION.

Growth of the " South Carolina Doctrine."

I. **Acts and threats of Nullification by the State.**

1817–1819. Ohio. Action of the State regarding the branches of the United States Bank.

1819. Lays a tax, defies an injunction of the Circuit Court of United States, and collects the tax by force.

1820. Outlaws the Bank and defies the Supreme Court.

1820, Dec. 20. Legislature adopts and reaffirms the " Virginia and Kentucky resolutions of 1798 and 1800."

Text of the Ohio resolutions

1822. Kentucky. The Circuit Court having enjoined her officers, and forbidden them to collect a tax levied on the U. S. Bank, the Legislature proposes a Constitutional amendment.

1824. New York.

Nov. 8. Resolutions approved in the Assembly on the subject of exacting tonnage duties from canal boats.

1825. South Carolina.

Reply of the Senate to Governor Wilson's message on the subject of the laws concerning free negro sailors.

1825. Protest against the tariff.

1827, Dec. Resolutions asserting the right of " interposition."

1827. North Carolina.

Memorial against the tariff. The tariff a " usurpation " of power.

1828, Dec. 19. Protest against the tariff, " the South Carolina Exposition " of Calhoun.

1828. Alabama.

Memorial of the legislature The tariff act a " palpable usurpation of powers."

1828. Georgia.

Reply of the legislature to the South Carolina resolutions of 1827.

1829. Virginia.

Reply of the legislature to the resolutions of Georgia and South Carolina.

WEBSTER–HAYNE DEBATE.

1. The Constitution a compact.
2. No common arbiter.
3. Respect for the opinions of other States.
4. The tariff unconstitutional.

1830. Mississippi.

> Feb. Resolutions concurring with those of Georgia, South Carolina and Virginia.

1830. Massachusetts.

> Feb. 9. Resolutions declaring that any act to put in force the decision of the King of the Netherlands would be " null and void."

1832, Jan. 19. Second set of resolutions

1831. Maine.

> Feb. 28. Resolutions to the same effect on the same subject.

1832, January. Second set of resolutions.

II. Webster–Hayne debate.

1829. Text of Foot's resolution on the public lands.

1830, Jan. 19. Hayne's first speech.

> 20. Webster's first reply.
> 25. Hayne's second speech.
>> 1. The South Carolina doctrine explained.

Jan. 26. Webster's Reply to Hayne.

1. " The South Carolina doctrine " examined.
   a. The right of a State legislature to interpose.
   b. This a constitutional and not a revolutionary right.
   c. Congress not the sole judge of its powers.
   d. The Supreme Court not the final arbiter.
   e. The States have a right to judge.
   f. The States have a right to nullify.
2. The South Carolina doctrine answered.
   a. Nullification revolutionary.
   b. The Constitution made by " the people," not by " the States."

NULLIFICATION.

  c. The Constitution and the laws supreme over State laws.
  d. " The probable *modus operandi* " of the nullifiers.
  e. The Supreme Court the arbiter.

1830, Jan. 27. **Hayne's Reply to Webster.**

  1. The right of interposition examined.
   a. The Constitution a compact to which the States are parties.
   b. How was that compact ratified ?
   c. What is the meaning of " We, the people."
   d. Who is the judge of infractions of the compact ?
    1. Is it the Supreme Court ?
    2. Is it Congress ?
    3. Is it the State ?
   e. What is the remedy ?
    1. Is it a constitutional amendment ?
    2. Is it interposition ?
    3. What constitute fit causes for interpretation.

1831, July 26. Calhoun's second manifesto.
   " Address to the people of South Carolina."

5. NULLIFICATION CARRIED OUT.

I. **Behavior of South Carolina.**

  1832, July 14. The Tariff Act passed.
   Oct. 24. South Carolina Legislature calls a convention.
   Nov. 19. The convention meet.
    Report of the committee of twenty-one.
   Nov. 24. Ordinance of nullification passed.
   1. Nullifies the Tariff Acts.
   2. Forbids the collection of duties imposed by such Acts.
   3. Forbids an appeal to the Supreme Court of the United States.
   4. Declares any act of coercion by the general Government null and void.

NULLIFICATION.

Address to the people of South Carolina.

1. "The Constitution is a confederacy."
2. "Who are parties to the compact?"
3. "The States, as States, ratified the compact."
4. "The States are as Sovereign now as they were prior to their entering into the compact."
5. To South Carolina therefore belongs the right to decide whether the compact be violated and what remedy the State ought to pursue.
6. The remedy is "nullification," "State interposition," "State veto."
7. Nullification "a natural right."

Address to the people of the United States.

The "Replevin Act."

The "Test Oath Act."

The bill to carry the ordinance into effect.

1833, Dec. 28. Calhoun resigns the vice-presidency.

II. Behavior of the President.

1832, Oct. 29 to Nov. 12. The troops put in readiness.

Nov. 6. Instructions of Secretary McLane to Collector J. K. Pringle.

Nov. 18. General Scott sent to Charleston.

Dec. 12. Naval vessels ordered to cruise near Charleston.

Dec. 11. Jackson issues his proclamation to the nullifiers.

Dec. 20. Governor Hayne issues a counter-proclamation.

III. Behavior of the "Co-States."

1833, Jan'y. New Hampshire. Resolutions.

Feb. 20. Maine. Report and Resolutions.

March 11. Massachusetts. Report and Resolutions.

Feb. 23. New York. Report and Resolutions.

Feb. 18. New Jersey. Resolutions.

1832. Dec. 20. Pennsylvania. Resolutions.

1833. Jan'y 16. Delaware. Report and Resolutions.

1833. Feb'y 8. Virginia. Resolutions.

NULLIFICATION.

Jan'y 5. North Carolina. Resolutions.

Feb'y 25. Ohio. Resolutions.

Ohio applies to Congress to call a Constitutional Convention.

Jan'y 9. Indiana. Resolutions.

Jan'y 12. Alabama. Report and Resolutions and Recommendations.

1. Congress to revise the tariff.

2. South Carolina to suspend the ordinance and not to use force.

Mississippi. Report and Resolutions.

1832. Dec. South Carolina issues a call for a Convention of the States.

1832. Dec. Georgia issues a call for a Convention of the States, and draws up a plan.

1833. Feb. Massachusetts disapproves of the Convention and answers South Carolina and Georgia.

Mississippi disapproves of a Convention.

1833. May. Connecticut. Resolutions.

Feb. Maryland. Resolutions.

Dec. Illinois. Resolutions.

IV. **Behavior of Congress.**

1833. January 16. The nullification message.

21. Force Bill introduced.

22. Calhoun's resolution on the powers of Congress. Grundy's resolution on the tariff and nullification.

L833, Feby. 15. Calhoun's speech.

1. Delegated or reserved powers.

2. The States have a right to judge of the extent of the reserve powers.

3. The Supreme Court not an arbiter.

4. Conduct of South Carolina defended.

Feby. 16. Webster's speech.

1. The Constitution not a compact.

DEFECTS IN THE CONSTITUTION.

2. No secession without revolution.
3. There is a supreme law or a final interpreter.
5. Nullification unconstitutional and revolutionary.

1833. The compromise.

6. PROPOSED AMENDMENTS TO THE CONSTITUTION,
1815–1832.

I. **Relating to the President.**

1816. To be chosen by the district system.
1818. The appointing power.

  1. President no power to approve or disapprove bills.
  2. Senate and House of Representatives to appoint all officers by joint ballot.
  3. Senate and House of Representatives to appoint all heads of departments.

1818. Five Sates recommend the choice of electors in districts.
1820. District system of choosing electors.
1821. Similar amendments.
1822. To divide the United States into four "Presidential sections."
1822. Concerning eligibility to the Presidency.
1823. Concerning the election of President.
1823. Long report on the subject.
1823–1824. Sundry amendments providing for choice of electors in districts.
1825. Effect of the failure to elect in 1824.
1825–1832. Amendments providing for choice of electors.

  A. 1. In districts with intervention of Congress.
     2. In districts without intervention of Congress.
     3. In districts with intervention of State Legislatures.
     4. In case of no election by electors, a choice by joint ballot by both Houses of Congress.
     5. In case of no election, an election by the people.
     6. By direct vote of the people.

  B. Providing for direct election by the people.
     1. Without intervention of electors.

DEFECTS IN THE CONSTITUTION.

   2. Per cápita rate over the United States.

   3. Direct popular vote in each State, the vote of each State being equal to its representation in Congress.

  c. Term of President.

  D. Eligibility to re-election.

  E. Recommendations of Jackson.

II. Amendments concerning Congress.

1816. Term of Senators.

1816. Power to remove judges by two-third vote of each branch.

1817. Congress and the States to have concurrent power to train the militia.

1817. The pay of Congressmen.

1818. The appointing power to be vested in.

1820. No power to charter banks except in District of Columbia.

1822. Pay of Congressmen.

1821. States to appeal from the Supreme Court to the Senate.

1823. Power to build roads and canals.

1823. Power to carry on internal improvements.

1824. Power to make roads and canals.

1825–1832. Powers of the House in case of failure to elect a president.

1826. Concerning the appointment of Congressmen to office.

1826. Congress to propose amendments every tenth year and no oftener.

III. Amendments Concerning the Judiciary.

1816. Removal of the Judges.

1826. Limiting the time of service.

1831. The same.

IV. Interpretation of the Constitution.

1823. Powers of Congress and the States over slavery.

JACKSON AND THE CONSTITUTION.

PART III., 1829–1837.

1. THE BANK QUESTION.

The struggle for re-charter.

1829, Dec. 8. Jackson attacks the Bank in his message.

1830, May 10. Resolutions declaring the House will not consent to a renewal of the charter.

    1. Congress no power to charter a corporation with authority to manufacture money out of paper.

1830, April 13. Report of Committee of Ways and Means.

    1. Has Congress power to incorporate a bank such as that of the United States?

        a. Precedent.

        b. Opinions of party leaders and action of the parties.

        c. Decision of the Supreme Court.

        d. Power to " coin money and fix the value thereof."

        e. States forbidden to coin money or emit bills of credit.

        f. Duty of the government to maintain a uniform currency.

1830, Dec. 7. Jackson refers to the Bank in his message.

1831, Feb. 2. Leave to bring in a bill to forbid re-charter refused by the Senate.

    Dec. 9. Jackson's message.

1832. January. Petition of the Bank for renewal.

    Debate on re-charter.

    1. Bank necessary to enable Congress to fulfil its constitutional obligations of

        a. Regulating the value of money.

REMOVAL OF THE DEPOSITS.

2. Proposition to permit each State to tax any branch set up within its borders.

   a. May Congress grant this power to the States.

   b. Have the States surrendered the taxing power except as to imports and exports ?

1832, July 2. Re-charter bill passed.

  July 10. Veto message of Jackson.

    1. Decision of the Supreme Court reviewed.

    2. Power of Congress to grant "exclusive privileges" discussed.

    3. Power of the Government to purchase lands within States.

    4. The Bank not " necessary."

     States have not given up the right to tax banks.

1832, July 11. Answer of Webster to the constitutional objections of Jackson.

  July 11. White, of Tennessee answers Webster.

2. "REMOVAL OF THE DEPOSITS."

1832, Dec 4. Message of Jackson on the deposits.

1833, March 2. House resolution declaring their safety.

  June 1. Duane made secretary.

  Sept 18. " Paper read to the Cabinet."

  Sept 21. Duane refuses to remove the deposits and (Sept. 23) is dismissed.

  Sept 29. Taney gives the order.

  Dec 3. Jackson's defense.

    Was the removal constitutional ?

1. The charter a contract.

2. The powers of removal discretionary with the Secretary.

3. The President had supervision over the acts of the Secretary.

The resolutions of censure.

1833. Dec 10. Clay's resolution relating to "the paper read to the Cabinet."

    12. Refusal of Jackson to send a copy.

JACKSON'S PROTEST.

1. President and Senate are co-ordinate branches of Government.
2. Knew of no constitutional authority of the Senate to call for such papers.
    26. Clay's resolution of censure.
1. The President in removing Duane had exceeded his powers.
2. The reasons of Taney for removing the deposits not satisfactory.

1834. March 28. Modified resolutions passed.
1. That the President has assumed authority and power not conferred by the Constitution and the laws.

   April 15. Jackson protests.
1. The resolution unauthorized by the constitution.
2. The resolution equivalent to impeachment.
3. The impeachment conducted in an unconstitutional manner.
4. Power of removal an executive power.
5. The Senate cannot meddle with the executive power.

1834, May 7. Senate resolution denying the right of protest.
1834–1835. State Legislatures demand the expunging of the veto of censure.

1834, April 17. Benton's notice.
1835, Jan. Alabama instructions.
   The doctrine of instruction.
   Resignation of Tyler of Virginia.

1837, Jany. 12. Debate on the constitutional question of the journal.
1. The resolution unconstitutional and ought never to have been spread on the journal.
2. Precedent.
    a. The old Congress.
    b. The Federal Convention.
    c. Massachusetts Senate.
    d. House of Representatives.
3. Meaning of the terms.
    a. "Shall keep."
    b. "Publish."
    c. "Proceedings."
4. Argument of the "yea and nay vote."

3. TENURE OF OFFICE.

Review of Jackson's removals from office.

1829, Dec.   Remarks on the subject in his message.
1830.   Debate on the tenure of office and power of removal.
1.   Is the power of removal an executive power ?
2.   Can it be separated from the power of appointment ?
3.   Action of Congress in organizing the departments.
4.   Action of former Presidents.
5.   Decision of the Supreme Court.
6.   " The expression of one tenure in favor of the judges is the exclusion of the like tenure as to all other officers.
1830, April 28.   Resolutions of Senator Holmes.
1.   May the President " remove during a recess of the Senate ? "
1832, Jan. 25.   Ewing's resolution.
1834, March 7.   Clay's resolutions.
1835, Jan. 5.   Calhoun's bill to limit executive patronages Constitutional question on the 3d Section.
1.   What is " executive power ? "
2.   Is the power of removal an executive power ?
3.   Is power to remove correlative to power to appoint ?
4.   Must the Senate share in the removing power ?
5.   The power not delegated and not incident to appointing power.
1835, Feby.   Bill passed by Senate.

4. THE "SPECIE CIRCULAR."

1836, July 2.   The Treasury order sent out.   Text of the order.
1837, Dec.   Motion to rescind the order.
          Constitutional questions.
1.   Has Congress power to rescind a treasury order ?
2.   Question of the " constitutional currency."
3.   Jackson's views.
4.   Does the right to lay taxes include the right to determine the money with which they shall be paid ?

PUBLIC LANDS.

5. DISTRIBUTION OF THE PUBLIC LANDS.

Resolutions concerning the use of public lands.

    1829. Dec. 29. Foot's resolution.

    1829, Dec. 17. Hunt's resolution for distribution of the net annual proceeds of sales among the States.

        1. Question of constitutionality.

            a. The lands " trust estate."

            b. The question of contract with the ceding States.

            c. The terms of the contract.

            d. Lands must go to the new States when the contract is fulfilled.

            e. Lands in Florida and Louisiana Purchase not pledged to pay the debt.

            f. May Congress own lands in the States except for the purposes mentioned in the Constitution ?

    1830, January 19. Resolution passes the House.

    1830, May 3. Benton's plan for graduated prices.

    1830, May 3. Tazewell's resolution to surrender to the States.

    1830, Dec. 7. Jackson's message.

    1832, March 23. Clayton's resolution to inquire into expediency of distributing the land and the proceeds of sales.

    1832. April 16. Clay's report and bill.

        May–July. Passed in Senate, lost in the House.

    1832, Dec. 4. Jackson's message.

        Dec. 12. Clay's bill reintroduced.

    1833, Jan. 25. Colonization amendment.

        March 12. Passes Congress and is pocket vetoed.

    1883, Dec. 5. The pocket veto discussed in the message.

        1. The contract theory of cession.

            a. Lands the common property of the States.

            b. Expressly accepted for this and no other purpose.

            c. Repeatedly pledged for payment of the debt.

        2. Constitution gives no power to abrogate the contract.

        3. Congress has no power to appropriate money for internal improvements.

        4. Tends towards " consolidation."

PUBLIC LANDS.

1833, Dec. 18.   Clay's bill reintroduced.
1835, Dec. 29.   Clay's bill reintroduced
    1.   The contract theory.
       a.   Congress cannot be a trustee.
       b.   The land a common fund.
       c.   No contracts with the States.
       d.   Congress may use *the land* as it pleases.
       e.   When the land is turned into money the revenue cannot be used for internal improvements.
1836. Dec. 19.   Clay's bill to distribute the proceeds of sales till Jan. 31, 1841.
1837, Feb. 9.   Calhoun's bill to cede to the States in which they lie.

SLAVERY AND THE CONSTITUTION.
PART IV.

—

1. SLAVERY BEFORE THE FEDERAL CONVENTION.

Part I. Pages 9 and 10.

2. SLAVERY BEFORE CONGRESS. (Part I., page 10.)

1792–94. Petitions.
1793. First fugitive slave act.
1797. Jan'y 30. Petition from kidnapped negroes.
1800. Jan'y 2. Petition from free negroes.
1802. Jan'y 2. Second fugitive slave act proposed.
1804 and 1806. Constitutional amendments offered. (Part I., page 16.)
1807. Slave trade forbidden.
1815. Hartford Convention amendments.

3. SLAVERY IN THE TERRITORIES.

1787. Ordinance of 1787.
  1. Territories in which the 6th article was enforced.
  2. Territories in which the article was suspended.
  3. Attempts to have the article repealed.
    a. Ohio.
    b. Indiana.
    c. Illinois.
    d. Michigan.
  4. Reports to Congress on the subject.
1819. Slavery in Missouri.

SLAVERY IN MISSOURI.

4. THE MISSOURI COMPROMISE.

I. **The First Compromise.**

1812–1819. History of the formation of Missouri Territory; the organization of Arkansas; the first and second admission bills; the coupling amendment; and the amendments of Trimble, Thomas, Storrs and Taylor.

1819, Feby. 13. Second admission bill.

Feby. 15. Tallmadge's amendment providing

1. That further introduction of slavery and involuntary servitude be prohibited.
2. All children born after the admission of Missouri to be free at the age of 25.

Question discussed.

1. Has Congress power to require such a constitutional prohibition of Missouri?

1819, March 3. Congress adjourns without action.

II. **The Act to Admit the District of Maine.**

1819, Dec. 30. Bill to admit Maine passes the House.

1820, Jan'y –. An amendment coupling the bill to admit Maine and Missouri offered in the Senate.

III. 1820, January 13. **The Coupling Amendment in the Senate.**

This coupling improper, because:

1. *The admission of Maine optional with Congress.*
   a. " New States may be admitted."
   b. New States cannot be formed out of old States without " the consent of the States concerned as well as of the Congress."
   c. Maine had obtained no enabling act.
2. *Missouri must be admitted.*
   a. The language and pledges of the treaty of 1803.

1820, Jan. 17. *Roberts' prohibitory amendment.*

SLAVERY IN MISSOURI.

The question of restriction debated.

1. May Congress lay any restriction on a State at the time of admission ?
    a. The guarantee of "Republican form of government."
    b. Power to make " all needful rules and regulations " for the territories.
2. May the Congress lay an anti-slavery restriction on a State as a condition of admission ?
    a. " The citizens of each State shall be entitled to all the right * * * of citizens in the several States."
1. The right of citizens to change their State Constitution.
2. The right of citizens to abolish or establish slavery by contitutional provision.
3. May Congress lay a restriction the citizens of a State can abrogate at pleasure ?
    c. " The migration and importation of such persons, etc., * * * shall not be prohibited prior to 1808."
    d. " Congress may admit new States."
    c. Power " to regulate commerce * * * among the several States."
3. May the Congress lay an anti-slavery restriction on Missouri as a condition of admittance to the Union ?
    a. The language of the treaty of 1803.
        1. " The inhabitants of the ceded territory shall be * * * * as soon as possible."
        2. " Principles of the Federal Constitution."
        3. " Rights, advantages and immunities of the citizens of the United States."
    4. The " property" guarantee.
1820–2, February 1. Roberts' amendment lost.
    16. Coupling amendment carried.
    16. Thomas's amendment to Missouri branch of the bill.
    16. Trimble's amendment to Thomas' amendment.
1820, Feby. 17. Thomas' amendment carried.
    Feby. 23. House rejects the Senate amendment.

SLAVERY IN MISSOURI.

V. The Missouri Bill debated in the House.

1820, January 26.   Storrs' amendment moved.
Taylor's amendment moved.

    I. The right of Congress to impose conditions discussed.

        a. Power over territories.
            1. When does a Territory become " a State ? "
            2. Congress may fix the boundaries of " new States."
            3. Congress may reserve land in " new States."
            4. Congress may prescribe that U. S. lands shall not be taxed, etc., by " new States."
            5. Precedents established.

    II. The right to impose anti-slavery conditions on Missouri.

        a. The rights guaranteed by the treaty.
        b. Is slavery a "principle of the Federal Constitution ? "
        c. Is slavery "a right of the citizens of the United States? "
        d. Was slavery guaranteed by the treaty ?
        e. The migration and importation clause.
        f. The regulation of commerce clause.
        g. The necessary and proper clause.
        h. The general welfare clause.
        i. Does power to admit imply power to prescribe conditions ?
        j. May Congress exact, as the terms of admission from "a new State," the surrender of political rights enjoyed by an "old State "?
        k. Has power to legislate on slavery ever been delegated ?
        l. Is it a reserved right ?

1820, Feb. 29.   Taylor's amendment passed.
   March 1.   The Missouri enabling Act passed by the House.
   March 2.   The Senate passed the House Bill with an Amendment.

ANTI-SLAVERY PUBLICATIONS.

I. THE FIRST COMPROMISE.
    1. The terms of the compromise.
    2. Views of Monroe.

V. **The Second Missouri Compromise.**
    I. 1820. Nov. 23. Report of House Committee on the Constitution.

    Missouri Constitution.
        Art. 3, Sec. 26. "That it shall be the duty of the General Assembly of the State, as soon as may be, to pass such laws as may be necessary, to prevent free negroes and mulattoes from coming to and settling in this State under any pretext whatever."
        1. Is this republicanism ?
        2. What is meant by "the privileges and immunities of citizens of the several States ? "
        3. Who may become citizens ?
        4. What has been the status of the negro in the different States ?
        5. Provisions of the naturalization law.

II. THE SECOND COMPROMISE.
1820. Dec. 11. Senate amendment passed.
1821. Feb'y. Attempts in the House to strike out the section.
        Feb'y 10. Report of Clay's committee with compromise resolution.
        Joint Committee appointed.
        Feb'y 20. Report of the Committee.
1821. August 10. Proclamation of Monroe declaring Missouri a State.

5. INCENDIARY PUBLICATIONS IN THE MAILS.
1835, Dec. 8. Jackson's message
        Select Senate Committee appointed to consider it.
1836, Feb. 4. ⁄ Calhoun's report and bill.
    1. Congress not power to pass a law forbidding the transmission of incendiary publications.

SLAVERY IN THE DISTRICT OF COLUMBIA.

2. No law to abridge the liberty of the press.
3. Congress has not a right to determine what papers are "incendiary."
   a. Such right would interfere with the reserved rights of the State.

Feb. 4. Text of the committee's bill.

1836, June. The bill violates.
1. The provision for freedom of speech and of the press.
2. The right of the individual to be secure in his papers.
3. Power to establish "post offices and post roads" does not give power to determine of what the mails shall consist.
5. The analogy of the alien and sedition laws.

1836, June. The bill rejected.

6. SLAVERY IN THE DISTRICT OF COLUMBIA.

1829–1835. Petitions for the abolition of slavery in the District.

1836, January 7. *Question of receiving raised.*

Such petitions unconstitutional because
1. Congress has no power to abolish slavery
2. Interferes with personal property.
3. Congress has no power to abolish slavery in the District while it exists in Maryland and Virginia.
4. A petition asking Congress to do an unconstitutional act is an unconstitutional petition.
5. In petitions for redress of grievances the grievances must be those of the petitioners, not of others.

The petitions must be received because
1. The Constitution provides for the right of petition.
2. Congress has exclusive jurisdiction of the District and would abolish slavery.

1835, December 31. Resolution of Mr. Owens.

1836, January 6. Resolution of Mr. Jarvis.
of Mr. Wise.
of Mr. Glascock.

"GAG RULE."

February 4. Mr. Pinckney. Petitions for the abolition of slavery in the District to be sent to a committee with instructions to report that Congress has no power to meddle with slavery.

February 10. Select Committee of nine appointed.

1836, Feb. 9 Protest against Pinckney's first resolution by three members.

May 18. Report of the select committee :

1. Congress no power to interfere in any way with slavery in any State of this Confederacy.

2. Congress ought not to interfere in any way with slavery in District of Columbia

May 25. First resolution passed, 182 to 9.

May 26. Second resolution passed, 132 to 45.

1837, Jan. 18. Mr. Hawes' motion that all such papers be tabled without being printed or referred, and no further action be taken, carried 126 to 69.

Feb. 11. Right of petition denied to slaves.

Atherton's Resolutions.

1838, Dec. 11. 1. The Government one of limited powers.

2. Abolition petitions indirect attack on slavery in the States.

3. Congress no power to do indirectly what it cannot do directly.

4. Congress has no power to discriminate between the institutions of the States.

5. Abolition petitions to be laid on the table without being read, printed or referred.

1838, Dec. 13. Six resolutions of Mr. Wise.

13. Resolutions of Mr. Adams on the powers of Congress.

1839, Jan. 14 Resolutions of Mr. Elmore defining the Constitution of the United States, and the relation of the Federal and State Governments.

RIGHT TO ANNEX FOREIGN SOIL.

1840, Jan. 28.   Resolutions of W. C. Johnson of Maryland. The
" Twenty-first Rule " adopted.

1844.   The " right of petition " debated.
Repeal of the " Twenty-first Rule."

7. SLAVERY AND THE CONSTITUTION.   THE ANNEXATION OF TEXAS.

I. 1836–1845.   History of the annexation movement.

1844–5.   Annexation resolutions.

1844, Dec. 4.   Recommendation of Tyler in his message.

          10.   McDuffie's resolution.

          12.   Benton's bill providing for.

               1.   The admission of " The State of Texas."

               2.   The formation of " The Southwest Territory."

Dec. 12.   [H. of R.]   Joint resolution to annex.

          23.   Weller [Ohio.]   To annex as a territory.
Motion of Hamlin to inquire.

          1.   Has Congress constitutional authority to annex a foreign
country ?

          2.   Would the annexation of Texas extend and perpetuate
slavery in the slave States, and has Congress power
over slavery in the States, either to perpetuate or do
away with it ?

1845, January 2.   Douglass [J. R.].   To re-annex the "Territory
of Texas."

1844, Dec. 31, Tibbetts.   Bill to admit Texas as a State with 36° 30'
clause.

January 6, Belser [J. R.].   To annex Texas as a Territory.

        8, McDowell.   Bill to annex the State of Texas.

        8, Dromgoole.   Bill to annex the State of Texas.

      13, Brown [J. R.].   To annex the State of Texas, with
36° 30' restriction.

      15, Burke.   Bill to annex State of Texas.

      22, King.   Bill to annex State of Texas, the State to
determine whether there should be slavery or no
slavery.

MANNER OF ANNEXATION.

II. CONSTITUTIONAL QUESTIONS OF

1. Annexation.
2. Re-annexation.

ANNEXATION. Discussed under

1. Annexation by treaty.
2. Annexation as a " State."
3. Annexation as a " Territory."

1. **By Treaty.**

   a. Texas foreign soil.
   b. Foreign soil only acquired.
   >   By discovery.
   >   By conquest.
   >   By coercion.
   c. Acquirement by cession or treaty power.
   d. Treaty powers belong to the executive not to the legislative branch.
   e. Congress cannot annex Texas.
   f. Congress can only act where the Constitution is in force.
   g. Constitution not in force in Texas.
   h. Texas must first be acquired by treaty.

1845. Feb. 4. Report of Archer. [Sen. Doc., 28th Cong., 2 Sess., Vol. 3, No. 79.]

2. **Annexation as a State.**

   1. Power to acquire territory not incidental.
   2. Congress has power to "admit new States."
   3. " New States" not a technical term.
   4. Means " newly made."
   5. Applies to the organization of government and not to the soil.
   6. Foreign States have been admitted to " this Union."
      a. North Carolina and Rhode Island.
      b. Vermont.

RESTRICTION OF SLAVERY.

7. Arguments drawn from the *Federalist* and the debates in the Federal Convention of 1787.

3. **Annexation as a Territory.**
   1. "New States" must be made out of territory within the limits of this Union.
   2. "This Union" means this government.

III. RE-ANNEXATION.

1. Texas a part of the Louisiana purchase.
2. Treaty of 1803 guaranteed incorporation into the Union forever.
3. Meaning of "incorporation."
4. Congress may part with soil but not with citizens.
5. The guarantee cannot be got rid of.
6. The cession of 1819 not constitutional.
7. Texas should be re-annexed.

IV. BEHAVIOR OF THE STATES.

1. Resolutions of the State Legislatures for and against the constitutionality of annexation.

V. THE COMPROMISE.

1845, Feb. Walkers' amendment to the House resolution.
1845, March 3. Tyler annexes Texas by joint rule.

SLAVERY IN THE TERRITORIES—THE WILMOT PROVISO.

1846. August 8. Proviso introduced and lost.
1847. February 12. Proviso reintroduced.
Question of constitutionality.

II. **Proviso unconstitutional, because :**
   1. The Constitution recognizes slavery.
      a. Art. 1, Sec. 2. Clause 3.
      b. Art. 1, Sec. 9. Clause 1.

RESTRICTION OF SLAVERY.

  c. Art. 1, Sec. 9. Clause 4.
  d. Art. 4, Secs 2 and 3.
  e. Art. 5.
 2. Congress cannot lay any restriction on a territory till it owns the soil.
 3. Slavery is a State, not a federal, institution, and cannot be established nor forbidden by Congress.
 4. " Regulation " does not mean " Prohibition."

1847. Feb'y 19. Calhoun's Resolution.
 1. The territories "belong to the several States," and are "joint and common property."
 2. Congress cannot make any law by which any of the States shall be deprived of full and equal rights in the territories.
 3. Any law preventing the citizens of any of the States migrating with their property to any of the territories would be such a discrimination.
 4. The people in forming a Constitution may form such government as they think best suited to their needs. Congress can enforce no restrictions as a condition of admittance into the Union save that it be republican in form.

II. The Proviso Constitutional, because :
 1. Congress has power to make all needful rules and regulations for the territories.
 2. Precedent.
  Ordinance 1787.
  Missouri Compromise Line.
  Oregon.
 3. Slavery a State institution and cannot be established, sustained or abolished by Congress.

SLAVERY IN THE TERRITORIES.—THE QUESTION OF RESTRICTION.

Theories of the right to establish or forbid slavery in the territories.

RESTRICTION OF SLAVERY.

I. Absolute power of Congress to govern.
1. Precedent.
2. Established by Missouri Compromise.
3. By restriction laid on " new States."

II. By " extending the Constitution."
1849. February 26, Walker's amendment to the Civil and Diplo-
matic Appropriation bill, extending the Constitution.
Debate on question, May the Constitution be extended by law ?

1. THEORY OF WEBSTER.
a. The Constitution does not extend to the territories, and
cannot be extended by law.
b. The territories are " *the property* " of the United States,
not " *a part* " of the United States.
c. This shown by action of Congress.
1. In establishing territorial courts.
2. In matters of internal improvements.
d. If the Constitution extends to the territories they must
be represented in House and Senate.
e. The Constitution extends over the States.

2. CALHOUN'S THEORY.
a. The Constitution the supreme law of " the land."
b. The territories are part of "the land."
c. Congress has no authority where its Constitution is not
in force.
d. Congress has power to legislate for the territories and
does legislate.
e. The Constitution therefore must extend or be extended
over them.

3. DRAYTON'S THEORY.
1. The Constitution does not extend to a territory.
a. The Supreme Court has so decided.

2   If the Constitution does not extend by its own inherent power
no act of legislature can carry it to a territory.

3.   To extend the Constitution to a territory is to make it a
" new State."

III. **By leaving the question to be decided by the Supreme Court.**

1848.   July 19   Clayton's bill from the Select Committee, providing
territorial government in Oregon, California and New Mexico.

1.   Slavery in Oregon to be left to the territorial Legislature.

2.   Slavery in California and New Mexico to the decision of
the Supreme Court when the cases arise.

IV. **By " squatter sovereignty."**

1847.   January 15.   The doctrine broached by Leake of Virginia.

1847.   December 14.   The doctrine set forth in Dickinson's resolutions.

1847.   December 24.   The doctrine more fully explained by Lewis
Cass in his letter to A. O. P. Nicholson.

V. **By carrying the Missouri Compromise line to the Pacific.**

1847.   January 15.   Burt's amendment to the Oregon bill lost.

August 10.   A similar amendment again lost.

August 10.   Douglas amendment, extending the line 36°
30' to the Pacific, carried and then rejected.

SQUATTER SOVEREIGNTY.

1849, Dec. 24.   President Taylor recommends it.

1850, Jan. 4.   Resolutions of Houston (Texas).

1.   Congress no power over slavery anywhere.

2.   Squatter sovereignty in territories south of 36° 30'.

1850, Jan. 21.   Taylor's answer to the House, defending his action
in California and New Mexico.

1.   Each State may change its Constitution.

2.   Slavery established or forbidden by State Constitutions.

RESTRICTION OF SLAVERY.

3. Useless to compel a State when entering the Union to adopt constitutional provisions that may afterwards be altered.
4. Question of slavery should rest with the people.

1850, Jan. 29. Clay's compromise resolutions.
  1. Text of resolutions 2, 5, 6, 8.

1850, Feb. 8. Foot's resolutions 1, 2, 3, 11.

1850, Feb. 28. Bell's resolutions providing for.
  1. "Popular Sovereignty."

March 4. Speech of McWillie.
  1. The North disregards the constitutional compact to return fugitive slaves.
  2. Congress no power to abolish slavery in the District of Columbia.
  3. Power over the District limited by the object and the nature of the grant.
  4. Abolition of slavery not an object of the grant.
     Because,
       1. Private property cannot be taken without compensation.
       2. No power to use the revenue for the purchase of slaves.
       3. No power to prohibit slavery in the territories.

1850, March 4. Calhoun's speech.
  1. Squatter sovereignty unconstitutional.
  2. Authority over the territories vested in Congress.
  3. People of California are rebels.
  4. Congress cannot *make* States, but only *admit States.* The State admitted must be a State before it is admitted.
  5. Calls for constitutional amendments.

1850, March 7. Webster's "Seventh of March" speech.

1850, May 8. Report of the Committee of Thirteen.
  August, Sept. The compromise carried.
       Squatter Sovereignty applied to
         1. New Mexico.
         2. Utah.

DEFECTS OF THE CONSTITUTION.

AMENDMENTS OFFERED.   1833–1850.

I.   CONCERNING THE EXECUTIVE.

1833.   Manner of election.
1834.   To be chosen by direct vote of the people in Districts.
1835.   Jackson's message on the subject.
1835.   To have but one term.
1836.   Jackson's message.
          Report of Committee.
1836.   Power of appointment and of removal to be taken away.
1836.   To have one term of six years.
1836.   No presidential electors.
1836.   ." *Viva voce*" vote of the people.
1836.   Direct vote of the people.
1837.   District election.
1838.   One term.
1840.   One term.
1844.   District election.
1844.   Direct vote.
1844.   One term.
1846.   Popular election.   Majority vote.   In case of disputed election a choice by lot.
1846.   One term of six years.
1848.   Direct vote.

II.   CONGRESS.

1836.   Majority vote to overrule a veto.
1836.   To appoint Secretary of Treasury.
          To determiné tenure of office.
          Members not eligible to office.
1838.   Not eligible to office.
1838.   Power to forbid and punish duelling.
1838.   Power to punish embezzlement with civil disability.

56

CONSTITUTIONAL AMENDMENTS.

1841.   1.   Majority to overrule a veto.
      2.   No more "pocket vetoes."
      3.   To appoint Secretary of Treasury.
1844.   Exclusive legislation over grounds and buildings in D. C., and over all lands bought for forts, etc.   Maryland and Virginia to legislate over the rest of District of Columbia.
1846.   Members not eligible to Presidency, Vice-Presidency, nor heads of departments of Treasury, War, State, Navy, Post Office, etc.
1849.   Senators to be chosen by the people.
1850.   Veto, tenure of office, disability of members.

III.   SLAVERY.

1839, 1.   No hereditary slavery of 1842, July 4.
      2.   No more slave States to be admitted to the Union except Florida.
      3.   No more slavery in the District Columbia, after 1845.
1843.   Massachusetts Legislature.   Representation and direct taxes according to free inhabitants.
1843.   Petition from Randolph and Washington counties, Ill., asking for an anti-slavery amendment.
1844.   Legislature of Massachusetts, to exclude slave representation.
1850.   Providing for "Squatter Sovereignty."

IV.   JUDICIARY.

1839.   Judges to hold office for a term of years.
1840, 1843, 1844, 1850.   Same amendment.
1850.   Removable in joint address of House and Senate.

V.   MISCELLANEOUS.

1838.   Duelling.
1838.   Embezzling.

www.ingramcontent.com/pod-product-compliance
Lightning Source LLC
Chambersburg PA
CBHW031752090426
42739CB00008B/987